Your Government:
How It Works

The Senate

Veda Boyd Jones

Arthur M. Schlesinger, jr.
Senior Consulting Editor

Chelsea House Publishers
Philadelphia

CHELSEA HOUSE PUBLISHERS
Editor in Chief Stephen Reginald
Production Manager Pamela Loos
Art Director Sara Davis
Director of Photography Judy L. Hasday
Managing Editor James D. Gallagher
Senior Production Editor LeeAnne Gelletly

Staff for THE SENATE
Project Editor Anne Hill
Project Editor/Publishing Coordinator Jim McAvoy
Associate Art Director Takeshi Takahashi
Series Designer Takeshi Takahashi, Keith Trego

The Chelsea House World Wide Web address is
http://www.chelseahouse.com

3 5 7 9 8 6 4 2

Library of Congress Cataloging-in-Publication Data

Jones, Veda Boyd.
    The Senate / by Veda Boyd Jones.
        p. cm. — (Your government—how it works)
    Includes bibliographical references and index.
    Summary: Discusses the history and duties of the United States Senate and presents a day in the life of one of its members.
    ISBN 0-7910-5534-5 (hc)
    1. United States. Congress. Senate—Junvenile literature.
2. Legislation—United States—Juvenile literature. [1. United States. Congress. Senate. 2. United States—Politics and govern-ment.] I. Title. II. Series.

KF4980 .J66 2000
328.73'071—dc21   99-048456

Contents

YOUR GOVERNMENT
HOW IT WORKS

Introduction

Government: Crises of Confidence

Arthur M. Schlesinger, jr.

FROM THE START, Americans have regarded their government with a mixture of reliance and mistrust. The men who founded the republic understood the importance of government. "If men were angels," observed the 51st Federalist Paper, "no government would be necessary." But men are not angels. Because human beings are subject to wicked as well as to noble impulses, government was deemed essential to assure freedom and order.

The American revolutionaries, however, also knew that government could become a source of injury and oppression. The men who gathered in Philadelphia in 1787 to write the Constitution therefore had two purposes in mind: They wanted to establish a strong central authority and to limit that central authority's capacity to abuse its power.

To prevent the abuse of power, the Founding Fathers wrote two basic principles into the Constitution. The principle of federalism divided power between the state governments and the central authority. The principle of the separation of powers subdivided the central authority itself into three branches—the executive, the legislative, and the judiciary—so that "each may be a check on the other."

YOUR GOVERNMENT: HOW IT WORKS examines some of the major parts of that central authority, the federal government. It explains how various officials, agencies, and departments operate and explores the political organizations that have grown up to serve the needs of government.

Introduction

The federal government as presented in the Constitution was more an idealistic construct than a practical administrative structure. It was barely functional when it came into being.

This was especially true of the executive branch. The Constitution did not describe the executive branch in any detail. After vesting executive power in the president, it assumed the existence of "executive departments" without specifying what these departments should be. Congress began defining their functions in 1789 by creating the Departments of State, Treasury, and War.

President Washington, assisted by Secretary of the Treasury Alexander Hamilton, equipped the infant republic with a working administrative structure. Congress also continued that process by creating more executive departments as they were needed.

Throughout the 19th century, the number of federal government workers increased at a consistently faster rate than did the population. Increasing concerns about the politicization of public service led to efforts—bitterly opposed by politicians—to reform it in the latter part of the century.

The 20th century saw considerable expansion of the federal establishment. More importantly, it saw growing impatience with bureaucracy in society as a whole.

The Great Depression during the 1930s confronted the nation with its greatest crisis since the Civil War. Under Franklin Roosevelt, the New Deal reshaped the federal government, assigning it a variety of new responsibilities and greatly expanding its regulatory functions. By 1940, the number of federal workers passed the 1 million mark.

Critics complained of big government and bureaucracy. Business owners resented federal regulation. Conservatives worried about the impact of paternalistic government on self-reliance, on community responsibility, and on economic and personal freedom.

When the United States entered World War II in 1941, government agencies focused their energies on supporting the war effort. By the end of World War II, federal civilian employment had risen to 3.8 million. With peace, the federal establishment declined to around 2 million in 1950. Then growth resumed, reaching 2.8 million by the 1980s.

A large part of this growth was the result of the national government assuming new functions such as: affirmative action in civil rights, environmental protection, and safety and health in the workplace.

Some critics became convinced that the national government was a steadily growing behemoth swallowing up the liberties of the people. The 1980s brought new intensity to the debate about government growth. Foes of Washington bureaucrats preferred local government, feeling it more responsive to popular needs.

But local government is characteristically the government of the locally powerful. Historically, the locally powerless have often won their human and constitutional rights by appealing to the national government. The national government has defended racial justice against local bigotry, upheld the Bill of Rights against local vigilantism, and protected natural resources from local greed. It has civilized industry and secured the rights of labor organizations. Had the states' rights creed prevailed, perhaps slavery would still exist in the United States.

Americans are still of two minds. When pollsters ask large, spacious questions—Do you think government has become too involved in your lives? Do you think government should stop regulating business?—a sizable majority opposes big government. But when asked specific questions about the practical work of government—Do you favor Social Security? Unemployment compensation? Medicare? Health and safety standards in factories? Environmental protection?— a sizable majority approves of intervention.

We do not like bureaucracy, but we cannot live without it. We need its genius for organizing the intricate details of our daily lives. Without bureaucracy, modern society would collapse. It would be impossible to run any of the large public and private organizations we depend on without bureaucracy's division of labor and hierarchy of authority. The challenge is to keep these necessary structures of our civilization flexible, efficient, and capable of innovation.

More than 200 years after the drafting of the Constitution, Americans still rely on government but also mistrust it. These attitudes continue to serve us well. What we mistrust, we are more likely to monitor. And government needs our constant attention if it is to avoid inefficiency, incompetence, and arbitrariness. Without our informed participation, it cannot serve us individually or help us as a people to attain the lofty goals of the Founding Fathers.

CHAPTER 1

An Exclusive Club

ON A COLD JANUARY afternoon, 100 senators, two from each of
the 50 states, sat at their desks in the United States Senate chamber of
the Capitol in Washington, D.C. The 100 wooden desks, most of them
antiques, were arranged in a semicircle, divided near the middle by an
aisle of rich blue-patterned carpet. On one side sat Republicans, and
on the other side sat Democrats. Senators had been assigned their
desks according to the length of time they had served in this legislative body. New senators, who had only been members of the 106th
Congress for a few days, could look inside the desk drawers for the
carved names of other senators who had sat at that same desk before
them.

A sudden hush fell over the senators and the people observing
from the chamber's galleries. Escorted by six senators, Supreme Court
Chief Justice William Rehnquist strode into the ornate chamber. He
stood rigidly in his formal black robe with the gold-striped sleeve as

he took the oath of the presiding judge of the Senate trial. He turned to the senators and began swearing them in as jurors that afternoon of January 7, 1999. One by one, the 100 senators answered aloud, walked forward, and signed a book, verifying their pledges to be impartial jurors in the **impeachment** trial of President Bill Clinton.

The nation watched as television cameras recorded the splendor, pageantry, and ritual in the Senate chamber on this historic occasion. None of the senators had ever participated in an impeachment trial of an American president. The only other trial was 130 years ago when President Andrew Johnson was acquitted. Few of the senators present had served as jurors in impeachment trials of court judges. Yet for many American citizens, this glimpse of the Senate reinforced their ideas of how senators work. But it is not an accurate view.

The pomp and circumstance of the Clinton impeachment trial (that ended with a not guilty verdict on the charges of obstruction of justice and perjury before a grand jury in a civil case) was unique. Roll-call votes on legislation, when senators answer "aye" or "nay" as their names are called, are few. More common are voice votes when senators for a measure answer "aye" as a group, and senators against a measure answer with one voice, "nay."

Andrew Johnson's impeachment trial by Congress in 1868 was the only other impeachment trial of a United States president. He was acquitted by one vote.

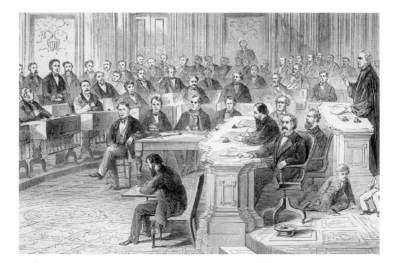

Most of the senators' work takes place not in the Senate chamber, but in offices and conference rooms. They work with staff members to draft laws. They talk with other senators in committee meetings to investigate elements of bills. They quiz presidential appointees for the president's cabinet or presidential nominees for judges.

Senators meet with people who represent special-interest groups, such as dairy farmers, labor unions, or tobacco industries. They talk with members of the press so that their ideas are reported on television and in magazines and newspapers. Senators pay special attention to citizens of their home states, because it is their job to represent them. People from their home states write letters, make telephone calls, and visit the senators in their offices in the Capitol to tell them how they feel about certain bills.

The Senate has changed throughout its history. The first Senate in 1789 had 22 members who were chosen by state legislatures. These men met in secret. Now the 100 Senators are elected by the voters of their states. Not only are sessions of the Senate televised on cable television, but special committee meetings are also on television.

Part of the day-to-day work of senators is meeting with special interest groups, such as these Greenpeace protesters who oppose new oil exploration.

In over 200 years, from the Senate's first session through the end of the 20th century, there have been only 1,851 senators. Most of the members of this exclusive club were men.

Only 26 women have served as senators. Eighty-seven-year-old Rebecca Latimer Felton of Georgia served for two days in 1922 as a result of a political appointment. Ten years later the Senate had its first elected woman senator. Although appointed in 1931 to fill the vacancy caused by her husband's death, Hattie Wyatt Caraway of Arkansas won the seat in her own right in the 1932 election. In 1996 a record nine women served in the Senate at the same time.

Just as the makeup of the Senate has changed through the years, the business and power of this institution have also changed. The Senate is only one half of the lawmaking branch of government. So that one legislative body wouldn't have too much power, the framers of the Constitution created two houses in the legislative department—the House of Representatives and the Senate. Historians agree that the original intent was for the House to be the main source of writing and debating bills and for the Senate to approve the bills. The Senate's primary duties were to advise the president, to approve treaties by a two-thirds majority vote, and to approve nominations by a simple majority.

Powerful senators—the great triumvirate of Daniel Webster, John C. Calhoun, and Henry Clay in the 1800s, and a century later, Lyndon B. Johnson, Hubert Humphrey, Everett Dirksen, Philip Hart, and Robert Dole—affected the Senate's development. The Senate's investigative role in important events like the Vietnam War and President Richard Nixon's Watergate scandal have also increased the Senate's influence.

In effect, the Constitution gives the Senate shared powers. Using the Senate's legislative powers, senators routinely introduce bills and debate their good points and bad

Henry Clay (standing, center) addressing the Senate. Although his three bids for the presidency were unsuccessful, he is considered to be one of the nation's most influential leaders.

points. As part of their executive powers, senators can approve or turn down presidential appointments or treaties. With their judicial powers, senators can confirm judges and act as the jury in impeachment trials.

The Senate has adapted to changes in the nation, but it likes traditions. Senators are proud of the antiques that adorn their chamber. Although they have interpreted and adjusted powers granted to them, senators take pride that the Senate still operates under the Constitution's guidelines, which were set forth over 200 years ago as part of a grand democracy.

The Constitutional Convention of 1787, with George Washington presiding, defined the structure of the new government and gave it the powers it needed to function as a nation.

CHAPTER 2

Compromise:
The Touchstone of the Senate

The First Senate and the Early Years

IN APRIL 1775, THE first shot of the American Revolution was fired in Massachusetts. This "shot heard round the world" signaled the beginning of the grand experiment in democracy. The entire federal government consisted of the Continental Congress, which was composed of representatives from the former British colonies. When the war ended, this one chamber ran the new country under the weak Articles of Confederation.

The federal government had very little power. It had no military force. It could not levy taxes. It could not regulate trade between states.

Power rested within the states. They maintained their own militias. Different states used different money. Each state regulated its own trade with other states, and some charged high taxes for goods coming into the state.

The nation's leaders could see that the confederation's loose system of government would not succeed. They called the Constitutional Convention in 1787 and began work on a charter that would create a more united country.

The leaders agreed on three separate branches of government: the executive, which is the president; the judicial, which is the court system; and the legislative, which is Congress. Should there be just one chamber in Congress as there was under the Articles of Confederation? Arguments flew back and forth. Small states like New Jersey wanted each state to have an equal number of representatives. Large states like New York wanted the number of representatives to be determined by the number of people who lived in each state.

Heated arguments gave way to cooler heads. A compromise was reached. There would be two chambers in Congress. In the House of Representatives, membership would be determined by state population. In the Senate, every state would have two members.

On September 17, 1787, the framers signed the Constitution, establishing the United States of America. When nine states had ratified the Constitution by June 1788, the Constitution became the law of the land. Two more states quickly joined the union.

Every state government had a copy of the Constitution and held elections for senators according to the provisions set forth in Article I. Section 3 stated that state legislatures would elect the two senators. (This was later changed by the Seventeenth Amendment, which allowed voters to elect their own senators.) Senate terms of office would last six years; but the terms would be staggered, allowing one-third of the Senate to be elected every two years.

The Constitution required a senator to be a United States citizen for at least nine years and to be a resident in the state where he was elected. Senators had to be at least 30 years old when they took office. The framers of the Constitution wanted mature men to make the laws.

For the first Senate, the new senators were to report on March 4, 1789, for the opening of Congress in New York City, which was then the nation's capital. But when that day arrived, there were not enough senators in town for a **quorum.** On April 6, when 12 of the 22 senators had arrived, the Senate convened.

The Constitution outlined Senate leadership. The vice president of the United States would serve as president of the Senate, but he could only vote in case of a tie. In his absence, a *president pro tempore* (from the Latin for "for the time being"), who would be elected by the senators, would preside. Because Congress had to count the electoral ballots for president and vice president of the United States, the Senate's first order of business was to elect a president pro tempore. John Langdon of New Hampshire was elected and presided until Vice President John Adams assumed his duties a few weeks later.

Then vice president of the United States, John Adams became the first president of the Senate in 1789.

The Constitution also defined the duties of the Senate. It would confirm presidential nominations and ratify treaties. It could introduce any bill except those dealing with money; those bills would originate in the House of Representatives. Although the House could impeach or charge a high public official accused of wrongdoing, the Senate would hold the trial.

Both chambers of the legislature shared power to borrow money, regulate commerce, coin money, establish post offices, set up lesser federal courts (other than the Supreme Court), collect taxes, declare war, and maintain the armed forces. The Constitution allowed the Senate the right to make its own procedural rules and required it to keep and publish a journal of its proceedings.

There was much work for the first Senate. They immediately took care of housekeeping details. They divided their members into three groups to set staggered terms. One group's initial term would be two years, another four, and the last group would serve the entire six years. After that, all terms would be six years. They set their pay at six dollars a day plus travel expenses. The first Senate set up three cabinet departments—the departments of war, state, and treasury—created the federal court system, and passed the first 10 amendments that form the Bill of Rights.

Many of the first Senate's decisions of protocol have become traditions. Because the Senate was to ratify treaties, President George Washington appeared before the Senate seeking advice on an Indian treaty. The senators held Washington in great regard. Many had served under the great military leader in the Revolutionary War. They did not feel comfortable debating an issue in front of him, discussing the pros and cons of his decisions. Washington expected immediate action, but the senators referred the matter to a committee. He left without an answer. Eventually the Senate offered an opinion on the treaty, but never again did Washington venture into the Senate chamber during debates. That tradition has been upheld by all other presidents.

Among the first Senate's order of business was to establish a federal district along the Potomac River for the nation's seat of government. While the Capitol was being built, the Senate moved its meeting place from New York to Philadelphia.

The Senate's membership expanded rapidly. In November 1789 North Carolina ratified the Constitution and its Bill of Rights. The new state was entitled to two members in the Senate. In 1790 Rhode Island became the last of the original 13 colonies to ratify the Constitution. Senate membership rose to 26. A year later, Vermont entered the Union, and two more senators took their places in the Senate chamber.

State legislators wanted to know how their senators were conducting business. They asked that the secret meetings be changed to open sessions so the press could report on the Senate debate. In 1794 the Senate complied. But it still met in secret to discuss treaties and presidential nominations for another 135 years.

Although political parties had not been formally organized, there were two distinct schools of thought in the first Senate. Some senators believed that the federal government should be very strong. All powers that the Constitution did not grant to the states should be given to the federal government. These men were called Federalists and rallied under the leadership of the first secretary of the treasury, Alexander Hamilton. Other senators felt that all powers that weren't specifically given to the federal government should remain with the states. These advocates of states' rights were called Democratic-Republicans, and their leader was the first secretary of state, Thomas Jefferson.

Immediately the Senate faced some issues that weren't addressed in the Constitution. Should there be a national bank? Alexander Hamilton convinced many congressmen that the bank was necessary for federal government operations. A national bank was established. What about protecting developing American industries with an import tax on

Federalist leader Alexander Hamilton, the first secretary of the treasury, believed that the new national government should assume all powers not specifically given to the states under the Constitution.

goods from other countries? Heated debate ensued, but the men favoring a strong federal government won the vote.

During the first decade of the Senate, a majority of its members were Federalists. They set up a strong federal government in the formative years of the new nation.

In 1800, with the election of President Thomas Jefferson, the Democratic-Republicans won a majority of seats in the Senate. The Senate met in the new Capitol in Washington, D.C., and entered a calm era.

The calm didn't last long. In 1812 Great Britain and France were at war. The United States remained neutral until Britain began stopping American ships that were trading with France. Soon Britain was seizing American sailors and forcing them into the British navy. Some senators demanded that the United States retaliate. Other senators wanted the country to remain neutral. President James Madison decided the United States should take a stand. He asked the Senate to declare war. On June 18, 1812, the declaration of war passed.

The war dragged on. In August 1814 British troops swarmed into Washington, D.C., and burned the Capitol. A year later, the British were defeated. The Senate conducted business from a temporary site until the Capitol could be rebuilt.

Traditionally, the Senate had set up temporary committees whenever an issue arose and needed study. Once

Two months after the Senate declared war on Great Britain in 1812, the USS Constitution *defeated the British warship* Guerriere *off the coast of Nova Scotia, earning prestige for the new United States Navy.*

the issue was dealt with, the committee would disband. Another committee would be set up for a different issue.

The problem was that the same powerful senators sat on all these temporary committees. A few men were running the Senate and deciding which bills would become the law of the land.

In 1816 the Senate set up its first permanent **standing committees,** including finance, foreign relations, and military affairs. Senators were appointed to committees for the length of each Senate term, which allowed long-term studies and investigations. Most senators stayed on their assigned committees during their entire Senate careers. Now senators became experts in certain areas; and powerful senators were not on all the committees.

The Missouri Compromise

The Senate was established by a compromise forming the legislative branch. One of its strongest moments was again to rely on compromise. In 1819 the country was growing westward. The Senate chamber made room for more seats as new territories prepared to enter the Union as states. Just as the first Senate had been divided over how strong the federal government should be, the current Senate was divided over the regional issue of slavery. Those from the South relied on slavery for their agricultural way of life. Those from the industrialized North saw slavery as evil.

The Senate was balanced equally between Southerners and Northerners. But now Missouri wanted statehood. Should it be admitted as a slave state or a free state? Debate raged on for weeks. Finally a compromise was reached.

Missouri would be admitted as a slave state, and, at the same time, Maine would be admitted as a free state. The balance between the North and the South would remain. In addition, the Senate decided that a line of 36°30' (36 degrees/30 minutes) latitude would divide the western territory. There would be no slavery north of the line, except for Missouri, but slavery would be permitted south of the line. The Missouri Compromise of 1820 established the Senate as a body of lawmakers who could overcome anger and hostility and work for the good of the nation.

The mood of the Senate entered an "era of good feelings." Most of the senators were Democrats. This party evolved from the old Democratic-Republican party of the early days of the Senate. Although the division between the North and the South remained, political parties didn't divide the Senate.

After the election of Andrew Jackson in 1828, the Senate became a place of bitter division once more. And the rift between the North and the South widened. At issue was a proposal allowing states to nullify federal laws that they didn't like. Of course, the issue behind the proposal was slavery. Northern senators opposed this challenge to federal authority.

Another dividing issue was the rechartering of the national bank that the first Senate had established. Although the Senate narrowly passed a resolution to recharter the bank, senators from the western states and the South thought the bank favored Northern industrial states. These

men, members of the same Democratic party as President Jackson, called for him to **veto** the charter. Jackson vetoed the bank.

For a brief time, anti-Jackson sentiment unified the Senate's most powerful men—Daniel Webster, Henry Clay, and John C. Calhoun. A new party—the Whigs—gained supporters, and within a few years they were a majority in the Senate. In 1834, during Jackson's second term, the Whig party had gained enough senators to **censure** the president for his stand on the national bank. Jackson became the only president ever to be reprimanded by the Senate. Still, he did not change his veto. A few years later, Democrats raised enough support to delete the censure resolution from the Senate journal. But they could not delete the hard feelings between the Democrats and the Whigs. The gulf in the Senate became wider and wider.

Andrew Jackson's victory in the Battle of New Orleans, 1815. His election to the presidency in 1828 was the beginning of an era of bitter political and regional divisions in the Senate.

Fall of the Alamo to Santa Ana's Mexican army in 1836. The question of whether slavery would be allowed in former Mexican territories immediately became crucial.

CHAPTER **3**

The Senate Gains Power

AFTER THE WHIGS OBTAINED a majority in the Senate and a Whig (William Henry Harrison) won the presidency in 1840, the party hoped to pass legislation that would strengthen the federal government. But President Harrison died after a month in office, and Vice President John Tyler took over the executive branch. Tyler was a moderate man who vetoed many Whig bills. Under his administration, political and regional divisions widened in the Senate and in the country.

The Compromise of 1850

The slavery issue would not die but gained strength as settlers moved into new western territories. The war with Mexico over Texas's boundaries brought slavery to the forefront once again. The House passed the Wilmot Proviso that stated that there would be no slavery in Mexican territories settled by Americans. The Senate defeated the bill.

In order to clarify the law as set forth by the Founding Fathers, John Calhoun offered a Senate resolution stating that the Constitution protected slavery. His resolution could not pass the equally divided Senate.

Henry Clay of Kentucky, known as the Great Compromiser, proposed a bill that might appease the North and the South. As with the Missouri Compromise, with one slave state admitted at the same time as one free state, Clay recommended that California become a free state and that the settlers of the New Mexico territory be allowed to vote on the slave question. He also wanted an end to the slave trade in the District of Columbia. For the South, he added a provision for a stronger fugitive slave law.

His colleagues, Calhoun and Webster, debated the bill from opposing sides. Calhoun loved the nation, but he was a Southerner from South Carolina. He feared that the South would secede from the United States if it was not given equal rights in the new territories. Daniel Webster of Massachusetts claimed he spoke not as a Northerner but as an American. He pleaded eloquently for the preservation of the United States. Clay warned the senators that they must take a strong stand or the Union would fall apart. He spoke in favor of the bill over 70 times.

Debate raged in the Senate with tempers heating up on both sides. At one point Senator Henry Foote of Mississippi pulled a gun on Senator Thomas Hart Benton of Missouri. Nearby senators jumped between the men. One wrestled the pistol from Foote. Others held Benton back. The president of the Senate pounded the gavel for order, men in the galleries shouted, and senators on the floor of the chamber rushed to keep the two men apart.

When order was restored, the Senate continued debate on the bill. Eventually it was passed, but it was not a resounding victory. The slavery issue in the territories had been side-stepped, not decided, by the Compromise of 1850.

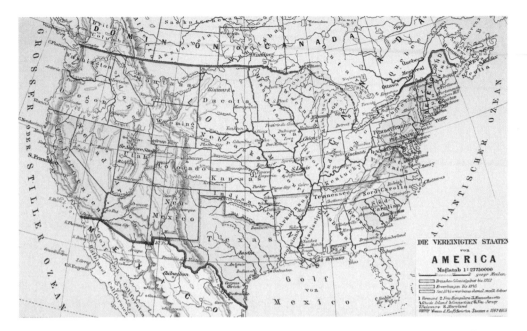

DIE VEREINIGTEN STAATEN
VON
AMERICA

The Kansas-Nebraska Act

Senators moved closer to a North–South confrontation four years later, with the passage of the Kansas-Nebraska Act. Both of these territories were north of the free state–slave state line drawn in the Missouri Compromise. If both territories were admitted as states, they would be free. The careful balance between free and slave states would be destroyed. Southern senators opposed the admission of these new states until the Kansas-Nebraska bill offered one more compromise. The citizens in those states could vote and decide the slavery issue for themselves.

Southern senators supported this bill because it gave slavery a chance to expand above the Missouri Compromise line. But Whigs and antislavery Democrats felt this bill was an attempt to spread slavery. Together they formed the Republican party and fought the bill. The Kansas-Nebraska Act passed, but the outcome was unexpected.

Most areas in Kansas were free, but there were some areas that allowed slavery. Violence erupted between slavery and antislavery groups. Marauding bands of outlaws

The Kansas and Nebraska territories were both located north of the line drawn in the Missouri Compromise to separate free states from slave states.

prowled the area, plundering and killing, all in the guise of defending or spreading their slavery philosophies. Fanatics in both slavery and antislavery factions called for retaliation in the name of their causes.

Violence again entered the Senate, the chamber where members called each other "honorable gentleman." Senator Charles Sumner of Massachusetts had given an antislavery speech about the violence in Kansas. In retaliation, two days later, South Carolinian Preston Brooks, a member of the House of Representatives, charged into the Senate chamber. He beat Sumner on his head with a cane, seriously injuring the senator. Words had failed to bridge the differences in opinion, and the "gentlemen" had given in to barbaric brutality.

The Secession of the South

With the addition of so many new states, bringing the total Senate members to 64, the legislative body had outgrown its old chambers. In January 1859 the senators met in the old chamber. Then in orderly fashion, two by two, they walked to the large new chamber in the new wing of the Capitol. This immediate need for more seats was short-lived.

After the election of Republican Abraham Lincoln as president, the Southern states knew their way of life was threatened. They feared that the spread of slavery to the territories would be halted. They also feared the passage of a tariff on imports that was favorable to the industrial North but harmful to the agricultural economy of the South. One by one the Southern states exercised what they saw as their constitutional right to secede from the United States.

In January 1861 Senator Jefferson Davis of Mississippi stood to bid farewell to his fellow senators and spoke for the Southern senators who believed in the right to secede.

I am sure I feel no hostility to you, Senators from the North.
I am sure there is not one of you, whatever sharp discussion

When Senator Jefferson Davis and senators from other Southern states that had seceded left the Senate in January 1861, the Republican party had a majority for the first time.

there may have been between us, to whom I cannot now say, in the presence of my God, I wish you well; and such, I am sure, is the feeling of the people whom I represent towards those whom you represent. I therefore feel that I but express their desire when I say I hope, and they hope, for peaceful relations with you, though we must part.

Davis led other Southern senators out of the chambers. Soon after, he was elected president of the Confederate States of America.

Left in the Senate were Republicans and antislavery Democrats. For the first time, Republicans formed a majority, and they lost no time in passing their legislation.

They declared war on the departed Southern states as the only way they saw to bring the United States back together. Then they raised money to support military forces by establishing an income tax, adding tariffs on imports, raising taxes on alcohol and tobacco, and allowing the government to print paper money.

Although the war raged around them, the mood inside the Senate chamber was peaceful because the senators, all antislavery men, were of like minds. They churned out important domestic bills. They gave public lands to establish colleges. They promoted the building of the first transcontinental railroad in the United States. They passed the Homestead Act, giving land to farmers in the western territories.

With the South's defeat, President Lincoln planned to bring the errant states back into the United States in a manner that would benefit all. But his assassination elevated Vice President Andrew Johnson, former Democratic senator from Tennessee, to president. Johnson had not seceded with his state and favored a lenient reconstruction policy.

Johnson irritated radical Republican senators, heady with victory, who wanted to punish the South for its rebellion. They overrode his veto of their reconstruction act. It divided the South into five military districts and set up guidelines for a state reapplying for U.S. statehood. When Johnson vetoed some of their civil rights bills, senators wanted revenge.

Senators' power lay in passing legislation. They passed the Tenure of Office Act, which forbade the president from removing any official whose appointment had required the Senate's consent. Johnson ignored the law. He felt Congress had overstepped its authority and was intruding on the executive branch's authority. He fired Secretary of War Edwin Stanton, a radical reconstructionist, who had been appointed by Lincoln.

Congress reacted quickly with impeachment charges from the House of Representatives. As the Constitution demanded, the trial was set for the Senate and required a two-thirds vote to convict Johnson. President Johnson held on to the presidency by only one vote.

The next few presidents after Johnson were weak. They'd seen the power of the Senate, and they did not challenge it. The Senate was now the most powerful body in the federal government.

The Senate's Golden Years

The 1870s and 1880s were golden years for the Senate. They wielded power, and with the power came corruption. The press had a heyday when senators attempted to raise their salaries by a whopping 50 percent. The public cried out against senators who gave federal jobs and contracts to their supporters. They accused some senators of selling their votes on important legislation.

In 1881 President James Garfield challenged the **patronage** system of civil service appointments. He made enemies, and not just among senators. An angry office-seeker who had been denied a civil service appointment assassinated Garfield.

Out of sympathy for the slain president, the public demanded civil service reform. The Senate finally passed a bill that protected federal employees from being fired for political reasons, but the law did little to undercut the power of senators.

By the turn of the century, the Senate had been nicknamed the Millionaire's Club. Its members were wealthy, and many people feared senators accumulated money through promoting themselves instead of doing their jobs. The public wondered whether they were working for the good of the country and its citizens.

To gain control over the senators, the states ratified the Seventeenth Amendment. Now senators would be elected by the voters in their states instead of by their state legislatures. Senators would be more accountable for their actions. If they didn't do what the voters wanted, the voters could vote them out of office.

Senate Majority Leader Trent Lott in his office in the Capitol building.

CHAPTER 4

Party Politics Define the Senate

The Early 1900s

BY THE EARLY 1900s the two-party political system of Democrats and Republicans was deeply rooted in the Senate. There were different schools of thought among each party: conservatives, who resisted change; and liberals, who sought reform. Still, parties were more organized than ever before.

On the Senate floor facing the front, Democrats sat at their desks on the left side, and Republicans sat on the right side. Those few senators elected from a third party or as independents chose on which side to put their desks. The dividing aisle moved as election results changed the balance of power in the Senate.

In the traditional conference held by each political party before a session began, senators elected a chairman and a party **whip.** The chairman became the party's floor leader. His job was to push the party's legislative programs. The party whip enforced party discipline and made sure senators were in the chamber for important votes. Both parties developed this type of leadership. The leader of the party with the greatest number of senators was called the **majority leader,** and the leader of the party with the fewest members was the **minority leader.**

Also at the party conferences, standing committee memberships were assigned and later approved by the entire Senate. Chairmen of the committees were usually senior members of the **majority party.** Because the finance and appropriations committees controlled the purse strings, they were considered among the most important committees. These chairmen became very powerful senators.

In 1912 Democrats won a majority in the Senate. They worked on domestic laws but were forced to focus on foreign affairs. In 1914 World War I broke out in Europe. When unarmed ships carrying Americans were sunk, the United States was drawn into the war. President Woodrow Wilson asked the Senate to declare war on Germany and the central powers.

When a German U-boat torpedoed and sank British passenger liner RMS Lusitania off the coast of Ireland in 1915, 123 American passengers on board died. American public opinion began to favor war with Germany.

When the war was over, Wilson proposed a League of Nations that would unite countries in an effort to prevent other wars. The League was part of the Treaty of Versailles that ended World War I. The Senate rejected the treaty, fearing the League would keep America from making its own foreign policy decisions.

After the war, Republicans won the majority of seats in the Senate. Many senators, along with many citizens, favored an isolationist policy of staying out of world affairs. They had seen how devastating World War I had been, and they wanted no part of a future war. Besides, there were troubles at home. By cutting taxes and raising tariffs, Republicans hoped to stimulate the sagging economy. These measures, however, weren't enough. The stock market crash in 1929 ushered in a long depression.

Finding that the Republicans had no solutions to the long food lines and few jobs, voters turned to the Democrats for answers. Democrat Franklin D. Roosevelt was elected president. He pushed his New Deal policies, and an eager Senate welcomed them. Many social programs were passed to get people back to work, with the government footing the bill.

World War II and the Postwar Years

While the Senate worked on domestic bills, Europe was undergoing drastic changes that culminated in World War II. The Senate, having seen that keeping the United States away from European affairs after World War I hadn't worked, sided with England and the Allies against Germany and the Axis powers. Senators passed legislation that provided aid to the Allies. After the bombing of Pearl Harbor, the Senate declared war on Japan and the Axis powers.

The war gained the support of the country, and the isolationist movement received a deathblow. The American people now knew that the United States could be attacked by a foreign country. America had to get involved in world affairs and work to keep peace between nations.

Greek, Italian, American, and British representatives of NATO countries pose on the guided missile ship USS Biddle. *The Senate's approval of the NATO treaty reflected its anti-isolationist mood after World War II.*

At the end of the war, the Senate moved forward in foreign affairs, and the United States joined the United Nations. Senators passed the Truman Doctrine, promising U.S. allies protection from communist takeover. They passed the Marshall Plan, which gave money to help European countries gain economic stability. They also approved the treaty making the United States a part of the North Atlantic Treaty Organization (NATO), a military pact between Western Europe and the United States.

The threat of communism hung over the world in the early 1950s. Communist China and the Soviet Union signed a friendship treaty. Communist North Korea invaded South Korea. The United Nations sent forces to that Asian country to fight Communists. People feared "the Red threat." Their fear was fueled by Senator Joseph R. McCarthy, chairman of the Government Operations Committee. Rumors of Communists in the government spurred his campaign to track down members of the Communist Party. He mainly targeted celebrities—actors, writers, and other politicians—and asked if they had ever been members of the Communist Party. He bullied innocent people, building his own reputation as he tore down the reputations of others.

Senator Margaret Chase Smith of Maine stood up against McCarthy and gave a speech against his ranting. She said that the Senate "has too often been debased to the level of a forum of hate and character assassination, sheltered by the shield of congressional immunity."

Most senators tolerated McCarthy's attacks on others. But when he attacked the loyalty of leaders in the U.S. Army, he went too far. The Army-McCarthy hearings were broadcast on a new invention—the television. A national audience was appalled by McCarthy's behavior. The Senate then voted to censure McCarthy for acting "contrary to senatorial ethics" and for bringing the Senate "into dishonor and disrepute."

Also in the 1950s, Senator Lyndon B. Johnson of Texas built a large group of supporters in the democratically controlled Senate. As majority leader, Johnson granted important committee assignments to those senators who supported him. His power grew as senators owed him for

President Lyndon B. Johnson signs the voting rights bill, part of his Great Society social reform program, into law in 1965.

putting them on the right committees. When he became president after John F. Kennedy was assassinated in 1963, he knew the legislative process and still maintained power in the Senate. He was able to pass his Great Society programs of social reforms by calling in favors. During this time the Senate established Medicare and worked to end racial discrimination by passing civil rights laws.

The Senate took giant leaps forward in domestic reforms but also kept an eye on foreign relations. Since the late 1950s the United States had kept an advisory force in Vietnam, where a civil war raged against communism. During President Johnson's administration, the conflict escalated. He asked for passage of the Tonkin Gulf Resolution, which gave the president authority to use force in Vietnam as necessary, even if it led to war. Only two senators, Wayne Morse of Oregon and Ernest Gruening of Alaska, voted against the resolution. Morse believed the Senate had made a great mistake. It had stepped around the Constitution and given what were supposed to be the Senate's powers to the executive branch. He said the senators "are in effect giving the President . . . war-making powers in the absence of a declaration of war."

As the number of ground troops and dead soldiers in Vietnam increased, senators reacted to public sentiment against the war. Soon the Senate was divided into two camps: doves, who were against the war, and hawks, who felt the war was justified. Many citizens loudly demonstrated against the country's involvement in Vietnam and blamed Johnson. He decided not to run for another term of office.

The Senate made its power known to President Richard M. Nixon, who also inherited the war. They repealed the Tonkin Gulf Resolution, and in 1973 senators passed the War Powers Resolution. It limited a president's right as commander in chief to send troops into combat without Senate approval.

A soldier going into battle in Vietnam. Many blamed President Johnson for the United States involvement in the war.

Party politics overwhelmed Nixon. His cohorts bur-
glarized the Democratic National Committee headquarters
at the Watergate complex. The Senate set up a special in-
vestigating committee to determine if Nixon was involved
in or covered up the break-in. When it appeared that he
would be impeached, Nixon resigned. Vice President Ger-
ald Ford became president.

The Senate flexed its muscles during the administra-
tions of subsequent presidents, much as it had a 100 years

President Jimmy Carter worked hard to convince the Senate to approve his treaties with Panama. The treaties established joint United States–Panamanian control of the Panama Canal until the year 2000.

earlier after the impeachment trial of Andrew Johnson. Senators had the power to bring down a president, and they did not let anyone forget that. The Senate curtailed the president's emergency powers and mistrusted executive decisions. Time and again the Senate rejected people nominated by the president for various positions—people whose nominations the Senate would have rubber-stamped 10 years earlier.

Believing that the nation needed a time of healing, President Ford pardoned Nixon. Ford felt a long drawn-out trial would dominate the country, keeping Americans from moving forward to more important matters. Many senators were offended by the pardon.

The Senate challenged many of President Jimmy Carter's ideas. Carter campaigned hard to convince senators that changes had to be made in Panama, a hotbed of unrest and anti-American feelings. The Senate deliberated six months before passing Carter's landmark treaties with Panama. The United States and Panama would jointly control the Panama Canal until the year 2000, when Panama would take over control. The United States kept the right to send troops to protect the canal against any external threat to its operation.

When Republican Ronald Reagan was first elected, the Senate was dominated by his party. He was able to pass many of his military programs. At the first hint of scandal, however, the Senate began an investigation. It uncovered a secret weapons deal between the United States and Iran. Profits from the sale of weapons were sent to rebel soldiers in the Central American nation of Nicaragua. Some of Reagan's top men were forced to resign because of the Iran-Contra affair. The president apologized to the nation for not keeping on top of his staff, but he survived the controversy.

Friction developed between President George Bush and the Senate when Bush violated the War Powers Resolution. He informed the Senate instead of asking their approval to send troops to the Persian Gulf. During Bill Clinton's term, the Senate turned down several of his cabinet choices and ultimately tried the president on impeachment charges.

The Constitution gave the Senate approval power on appointments and treaties and the power to declare war to keep a check on the chief executive. Over the years, the Senate has proved it isn't afraid to say no to a president.

Former New Jersey senator Bill Bradley at the headquarters of his campaign for the year 2000 Democratic presidential nomination. Since retiring from the Senate in 1995, Bradley continued to be politically active by bringing his support for various domestic and international issues to the private sector.

CHAPTER 5

Senator X Sponsors a Bill

A SENATOR'S LIFE IS very busy. He or she may start the day with a breakfast meeting and not end the day until after a late political fundraising dinner. It's not a life for someone who likes to be relaxed. It's an exciting, never-a-dull-moment life of public service.

What kind of person becomes a senator and how does he or she become a member of that exclusive club? Senator X represents the typical senator.

Senator X has always had political leanings. When he was in high school, he was on the debate team and was vice president of the student body. After college and law school, he worked as a public defender for two years. During that time, he became a card-carrying member of the Democratic party. Then he decided the time was right to run for public office. He filed for county attorney and won by a landslide.

Two years later he campaigned for a seat in the state legislature. Three other Democrats filed for the seat, so he faced several opponents in the August primary. He won handily and also beat his Republican opponent in November's regular election.

When the legislature met, he lived in the state capital. Senator X set up his own law practice in his district for the months the legislature wasn't in session. He continued to work for the Democratic party, and four years later he ran for the House of Representatives. He served there for eight years before winning a Senate seat.

Senator X has traveled the political path of many senators. Almost a third of today's senators are first elected to the House. Several former governors become senators, and a few senators are elected because of their celebrity status as athletes or actors. Senator X has his eye on the White House. Not since Nixon's election has a former senator become president; but Senator X figures it's time, and he works toward that goal.

Senator X is allowed a certain amount of money for staff salaries, based on the population of his state. Because there has been corruption in the past, the Senate passed rules that said no relative of a senator could work in his office. Senator X avoids any hint of wrongdoing. One of his voters gave him a framed cross-stitch that reads, "Power corrupts and absolute power corrupts absolutely." He hung it on his office wall as a reminder that he is a servant of the people and shouldn't get overly impressed with his power.

To his new office, he brought a staff of 40 people. Although most of these aides worked on his election campaign or served on his House staff, he made sure that they were all trustworthy and qualified for their jobs.

Senator X attended the long orientation sessions on how the Senate worked. He chose one of the available

desks on the left side of the middle aisle and carved his
name inside a drawer. He was proud that the famous de-
bater Stephen A. Douglas had once sat at his desk.

At the Democratic party conference before the annual
session began, he received his committee assignments. He
was placed on the standing committees for Banking, Hous-
ing and Urban Affairs; Small Business; Health, Education,
Labor and Pensions; and the select committee on Ethics.

Senator X has one aide for each committee. He also
assigned various members of his staff to research areas for
these committees and other pending legislation. When he's
called to the Senate floor for a vote, an aide meets him out-
side the chamber and gives him concise information about
the bill so Senator X can make a good decision. Other aides
in his office create reports and write speeches. Some at-
tend subcommittee meetings for him while he's in other
meetings.

Maintaining good relations with people from his home
state takes a lot of Senator X's time. Letters pour into his
office, and he requires his staff to respond to every one of
them. Some he answers himself, and he signs them all. Because members of his home state come to Washington for
vacations and want to meet with him, he set up a breakfast
for constituents. Every Wednesday that the Senate is in
session, he visits with the out-of-towners from 8:15 to
9:00 A.M., while coffee, juice, donuts, and bagels are
served in his office in the Hart Senate Office Building.
He's found that a set time to see constituents helps free up
the rest of his day for Senate business.

There were so many requests from his home state for
flags that had flown over the Capitol, that his staff set up
guidelines for ordering and payment. His aides in the five
offices he maintains in his state read countless newspapers
and cut out articles about his constituents and send these
constituents copies of the articles. These aides also deal

with constituent problems, many concerning Social Security. Senator X wants people from his home state to know that he cares about them.

He flies home twice a month and speaks to groups across the state to show them he's working for them. He also attends fund-raising events for his re-election campaign. Always with the next election and public relations in mind, he jumps at the chance to appear on issue talk shows like *Meet the Press* and *Face the Nation.*

Senator X's main job is to make laws for the people. He has proposed a bill establishing special schools for students who are at risk of dropping out of high school. He wants to keep them in a school environment, where they can achieve at their levels.

He sent the bill to the legislative counsel, which put the bill in proper form with carefully worded legal language. He then took the bill to the other senator from his state and to four other senators who were interested in the bill. He talked to these senators in the Democrats' cloakroom, a large room next to the Senate chamber where senators can talk in an informal setting. Three senators were willing to cosponsor the bill, with Senator X being the main sponsor. Another senator, with whom he works out in the Senate gym, also agreed to cosponsor the bill.

At a morning session of the Senate, Senator X rose from his desk. He introduced the bill and asked that the remainder of his remarks be inserted in the *Congressional Record.* The bill was given a number, S-63, by the legislative clerk, and the parliamentarian referred it to the Health, Education, Labor, and Pensions Committee.

Although Senator X spoke for only one and a half minutes, the speech printed in the *Congressional Record,* covered a full eight pages. It explained his reasons for wanting the bill passed.

In the committee meeting, the chairman of the committee assigned the bill to a subcommittee. Of the other

18 bills referred to the committee that day, only four others were assigned to subcommittees. The other bills did not win a position on the committee's agenda and died. No other action would be taken on them.

Senator X's bill was scheduled for discussion five weeks later. Senator X asked his staff members to round up witnesses willing to testify at hearings. A leading educator from his home state traveled to Washington, D.C., to present the state-funded at-risk program used at home. It had been successful in cutting the dropout rate. Several counselors and two teachers also testified. Subcommittee members asked questions of these witnesses, but the bill actually met with little opposition. The subcommittee voted to send the bill to the entire committee.

A full agenda in the committee kept S-63 from any immediate action. For eight weeks it received no attention, then it was presented to the committee. Senators marked up the bill, made a couple revisions, and scheduled it for a final reading a few weeks later.

In his monthly newsletter to the voters of his home state, Senator X headlined his bill. The article said that his state could lead the nation in showing how to cut the high school dropout rate. The cost of mailing this newsletter was covered under the franking privilege of the Senate, which allows Senator X to mail postage-free.

He courted the teachers' unions for backing. Aides wrote articles for teachers' magazines. Members of the union wrote letters to their senators urging passage of the bill.

Senator X talked to other senators in the committee about the bill. In the spirit of Senate compromise, he promised to vote for another senator's bill if that senator would vote for his. The other bill was one he believed in anyway, so he didn't feel he was trading his vote.

The committee voted on the bill and approved it. Next, S-63 went to the full Senate. Senator X had hoped for a

unanimous consent agreement and was disappointed when another senator proposed an amendment to require special certification for teachers of at-risk students. After some debate, the amendment passed with a voice vote. Then the entire bill was voted on and passed.

Next, S-63 went to the House of Representatives. Again, it was referred to committee. Senator X kept tabs on the bill through a couple of representatives from his state. It passed the committee with an amendment and then passed the House. Since it was now a different version of the bill than the one the Senate passed, it was referred to a conference committee, composed of members of both houses. Senator X was named to that committee.

The House had added a section on special classes for gifted students. Senator X was pleased with the amendment. After it was slightly rephrased, Senator X urged passage. The conference committee passed the bill. Once again the bill went to the floor of the Senate, and at the same time it went back to the House. Both chambers passed the bill. Now it awaited the president's approval or veto.

The president has ten days to veto a bill while the Senate is in session or the bill becomes a law. If he vetoes the bill, congressional leaders can schedule it for another vote. If both houses pass it by a two-thirds majority, the bill becomes a law without the president's signature. This legislation was something the president supported, and he invited key members of the Senate and House to watch him sign the bill. Senator X attended the ceremony and had pictures taken to put in the next newsletter to his constituents. He wanted them to know his record and remember it at election time.

He had the ceremony videotaped by the Senate Recording and Photographic Studio, and a few minutes later he added a two-minute introduction. The video was immediately sent via satellite to 25 TV stations in his state.

Now that the bill had passed, it had to be funded through an appropriations bill. Once S-63 had money behind it, a government agency would administer the at-risk program to the states.

Other bills Senator X sponsored or cosponsored did not fare as well as S-63. Many died in committee. Others were defeated on the Senate floor. He was not discouraged. Having one bill pass was a victory. Of the thousands of bills introduced in the Senate each session, only one-sixth of them make it on a committee's agenda and even fewer become laws.

President Clinton signs a bill into law in the Rose Garden of the White House. Supporters of the bill stand behind him.

The United States Capitol building in Washington, D.C. A new Congress convenes here every two years.

CHAPTER **6**

Today's Senate

WHEN VICE PRESIDENT JOHN Adams called the first Senate to order, tradition says he pounded on his desk with a small silver-capped ivory gavel. That gavel was used until 1954 when it had deteriorated so badly that it could not be fixed.

That same year the government of India gave the Senate a new gavel, an exact replica of the old one. Today, before each new session of the Senate, a case holding both the old and the new gavels is placed on the vice president's desk. The new one is used, but the old one stays on the desk, showing that the grand experiment in democratic rule still works.

How the Senate Functions

Although the vice president of the United States ceremoniously calls the Senate to order on opening day of the session, he does not normally preside. This chore should fall to the president pro tempore, usually the senior member of the majority party. Many times this is a figurehead position. Other members of the majority party take turns presiding over the Senate.

A new Congress convenes every two years. This occurs after all the members of the House of Representatives and a third of the senators have been elected. There are not 33 new senators every two years. Many of the senators are reelected. Of the 34 senators elected in 1998, most were **incumbents.** Only seven were elected to their first terms.

Unless the previous Congress has by law set a different date, the Senate convenes a new session on January 3. Most sessions run through November to mid-December with a month-long summer recess. The Congresses are numbered beginning with the first one in 1789. In January 2001 the 107th Congress will meet; in January 2003 the 108th Congress will convene.

After the senators are sworn in, they elect officers who are not senators. Normally these officers continue from Congress to Congress. The secretary of the Senate has both legislative and administration functions, and is in charge of clerks, payroll, and the maintenance of senate records.

The sergeant at arms's roll in the first Senate was to guard the door, because the senators met in private until 1794. Now this officer serves as chief of law enforcement and manages most support systems, including pages, galleries, the photographic studio, and the computer center. He is responsible for escorting the senators as a body to joint sessions of Congress and inaugurations.

The Senate chaplain offers a prayer at the opening of each daily session. He also serves as spiritual counselor for senators, their families, and their staff members.

The legislative counsel is a group of lawyers who assist in wording bills and resolutions. The legal counsel is composed of lawyers who represent senators in any legal suit related to their official roles. Both groups are considered officials of the Senate.

Serving their respective political parties are majority and minority secretaries. These officials oversee the cloakrooms and assist with the record-keeping side of appointing senators to committees.

In the early years of the Senate, powerful senators served on several committees and in this way increased their power. For a more democratic system, today's Senate has adopted specific rules about committee memberships. In 1999 there were 24 committees, consisting of 17 standing committees, 4 special and select committees that are set up for specific purposes, and 3 joint committees that have members from both houses.

Standing committees are divided according to their importance into Class A, Class B, and Class C. Senators may serve on only two Class A committees and one Class B committee. There is no limit to their membership on

House Speaker Newt Gingrich (seated, left) and Senate Majority Leader Trent Lott (seated, right) sign the IRS reform bill.

Class C committees. For each of the Class A and Class B committees, a senator is allowed a professional staff member who provides clerical and research assistance.

In a further attempt to equalize the role of senators, changes have been made to Senate rules. Instead of the chairperson being the senior senator, members are allowed to vote by secret ballot for the chairperson, whose term as chairperson is now limited to six years.

Across the nation, a push has been made for a two-term limit for senators. Several senators have been elected who promised to vote for term limits, and then they have changed their mind. They complain that it takes time to learn the system and attain membership on committees where they can influence legislation. They have filed for election again and again, and many have been returned to the Senate. Those who favor term limits claim that if terms were limited, senators would not have to respect the wishes of their campaign supporters or accept money from special-interest groups.

Special-Interest Groups

Many political action committees (PACs) contribute campaign funds to candidates who favor their special programs. These interest groups hire professionals to convince senators to support their causes. The representatives of these interest groups would try to waylay senators in lobbies as senators came out of meetings. Because the representatives might hang around the lobby for hours awaiting a few minutes of time with a senator, they became known as **lobbyists.**

Although many citizens believe that a lobbyist's job is to buy a senator's vote with money or vacations, that isn't the lobbyist's purpose. Because of bribery and corruption in the past, a monetary limit to any gift that a lobbyist can give a senator has been established. The law also sets a campaign contribution limit.

631253M

Many lobbyists target senators who already believe in their causes and they present them with services. Lobbyists may provide factual material or speeches. This frees up time for senators or their aides. Of course, lobbyists hope senators will convince other senators on their committee to support their issues. Yes, their views are biased. But so are the views of the lobbyists who present the other side of the issues to other senators on the committee. In committee debate senators can present both sides of the question, weigh the matter, and vote as informed senators.

Citizen lobbyist Katherine Prescott (left), the national president of Mothers Against Drunk Driving, looks on as First Lady Hillary Clinton opens a new antidrunk-driving campaign.

Senators may request specific information from a lobbyist. They may want a bill drafted by the special-interest group or have witnesses provided at a hearing. They may want advice on legislative tactics and help building support for the bill from the public and especially from the people of their home state.

But does a senator feel an obligation to vote for a PAC's interest if that PAC has helped get him or her elected? Probably. Could a senator be elected without campaign money from PACs? It would be most difficult because of the enormous cost of campaigns. The relationship between PACs and senators has created a huge dilemma.

Many critics of the Senate believe reforms in campaign laws could solve the problem of lobbyists buying influence from senators. But they believe senators will not willingly reform a system that works for them. Not waiting for national reforms, several states have passed laws setting up publicly funded campaigns.

The Clean Election Act, passed in Maine in 1996, gives candidates for state representative, senator, or governor a choice. A candidate can raise private funds with reduced limits or accept public funds. Campaigns cannot be launched until election year. This plan goes into effect in 2000. Its supporters believe it could be a pattern for national use.

The public has also criticized senators for the special perks they receive. Some cry foul at the allowance for foreign travel. Others believe the franking privilege (postage-free mailing) gives an incumbent senator an unfair advantage. He can send out bulletins free of charge that will cost another candidate lots of money.

Some people dislike the gym in the Dirksen Senate Office Building. Should a senator have a private workout place? Many senators use the facilities as a break from the pressures of work. In the privacy of the senators' gym, they are free from meeting and greeting those who would like to influence them. After a day on the Hill, as the Capitol area is known, they may relax in the steam room and get energized for evening meetings or dinner functions. They could be regrouping to go back to the Senate floor if a bill is being **filibustered.**

The Filibuster

Although the House of Representatives has disallowed filibustering, it is a time-honored right in the Senate. This practice of talking on and on against a bill allows the minority to block the vote until the majority compromises on the bill or drops it entirely.

There have been changes to this right to unlimited debate. The current rule allows a three-fifths majority, or 60 senators, to vote for **cloture.** This stops a filibuster.

During a filibuster one person may speak for a lengthy period of time, as Senator Strom Thurmond did for over 24 hours in 1957. Several senators may take turns speaking. Sometimes they address something other than the bill under consideration. One senator read Shakespeare and recipes to fill his filibuster time. Still others call for the reading of a day's worth of the *Congressional Record* in its entirety, which may be several hundred pages.

The majority leader may handle a filibuster in two ways. He can divide the Senate day in half and use one part for the filibuster and the other part for other legislation. This tactic keeps Senate business moving, although the filibustered bill is stalled. The majority leader may choose to keep the Senate in session until late in the night or not to adjourn until the filibuster is ended.

All senators do not stay on the floor during a filibuster. During an all-night filibuster, some may take naps in their offices. Others may head for the gym. Still others may go to a restaurant in one of the three Senate office buildings. Buzzers and lights alert senators when a quorum is called or a vote is scheduled. Tunnels and subways link the office buildings with the Capitol, so senators may return to the chamber in a timely fashion.

Filibustering should be used as a last-ditch effort to block a bill. Most senators would rather rely on persuasion, reason, or compromise to win other senators' votes.

Many senators wage a private debate. Were they elected to vote what the people in their home states want? They are a direct link between national government and the people. That is an important connection that should keep government responsive to the people.

Or were they elected to vote their own opinions? Their own decisions are based on information not always available to the home folks. Senators have heard testimony from experts. They should see the big, national picture rather than only what is important to their own states. Many senators feel they must vote their consciences.

Either way, most senators want what is best for the country. They know that many times they must compromise their own views to reach that end.

Glossary

Censure—An official reprimand.

Cloture—A movement to end a filibuster, or close debate; 60 senators must vote to close debate.

Filibuster—Unlimited debate to keep a bill from being brought to a vote on the Senate floor.

Impeachment—The charging of a president, vice president, or other civil official with a high crime. The House of Representatives makes the charge, and the Senate acts as the jury as the case is tried.

Incumbent—The person who currently holds an office.

Lobbyist—A representative of a special-interest group who tries to influence the way a senator votes.

Majority leader—The senator who has been elected by the controlling party to be the floor leader; this senator is the most powerful member of the Senate.

Majority party—The political party that has the most members in the Senate. (In the 106th Congress, 1999–2001, the Republican party was the majority party in the Senate.)

Minority leader—The senator who has been elected by the party with the fewest members in the Senate.

Patronage—The right to appoint a person to a job in government.

Quorum—The minimum number of senators needed to conduct business; 51 senators are necessary for a quorum.

Standing committee—A permanent committee concerned with a specific area of legislative issues.

Unanimous consent agreement—A vote to approve a bill without putting it on the Senate calendar for debate.

Veto—The power to keep a bill from becoming a law.

Whip—A party member who assists the party leader by organizing legislative business.

Further Reading

Congressional Quarterly. "How Congress Works." Washington, D.C.: Congressional Quarterly Books, 1998.

Feinberg, Barbara Silberdick. *Term Limits for Congress?* New York: Twenty-First Century Books, 1996.

Fireside, Bryna J. *Is There a Woman in the House . . . or Senate?* Chicago: Albert Whitman, 1993.

Harris, Fred R. *Deadlock or Decision: The U.S. Senate and the Rise of National Politics.* New York: Oxford University Press, 1993.

Heath, David. *The Congress of the United States.* Minneapolis, MN: Capstone Press, 1999.

Hernon, Joseph Martin. *Profiles in Character: Hubris and Heroism in the U.S. Senate, 1789–1990.* Armonk, NY: M.E. Sharpe, 1997.

Kronenwetter, Michael. *The Congress of the United States.* Springfield, NJ: Enslow Publishers, 1996.

Woodward, Bob. *Shadow: Five Presidents and the Legacy of Watergate.* New York: Simon & Schuster, 1999.

Website

The official Web site of the U.S. Senate:
www.senate.gov

Index

ABOUT THE AUTHOR: Award-winning author Veda Boyd Jones has written 23 books, including children's historical novels, children's biographies, a picture book, romance novels, and a coloring book. Other published works include over 150 articles and stories in children's magazines, adult magazines, and reference books. Jones earned an MA in history at the University of Arkansas and currently teaches for the Institute of Children's Literature. She and her husband, Jimmie, have three sons, Landon, Morgan, and Marshall.

SENIOR CONSULTING EDITOR Arthur M. Schlesinger, jr. is the leading American historian of our time. He won the Pulitzer Prize for his book *The Age of Jackson* (1945) and again for *A Thousand Days* (1965). This chronicle of the Kennedy Administration also won a National Book Award. Professor Schlesinger is the Albert Schweitzer Professor of the Humanities at the City University of New York, and has been involved in several other Chelsea House projects, including the REVOLUTIONARY WAR LEADERS and COLONIAL LEADERS series.

Picture Credits